BRIAN FLERAN &
R THE

THE
RESILIENCE
BOOKLET

**HOW EXTREME SURVIVORS
OVERCOME MASSIVE CHALLENGES**

The Resilience Booklet is a book written and based upon the real-life experiences of the author. In practical advice books, as in life, there are no guarantees and readers are cautioned to rely on their own judgment concerning their individual circumstances and to act accordingly.

Limit of Liability/Disclaimer of Warranty: While the publisher and author have used their best efforts in preparing this book, they make no representations or warranties with respect to the accuracy and completeness of the contents of this book and specifically disclaim any implied warranties of merchantability or fitness for a particular purpose. No warranty may be created or extended by sales representatives or written sales materials. The advice and strategies contained herein may not be suitable for your situation. The author and publisher are not engaged in rendering professional, legal or medical services, and you should consult a professional where appropriate. The author and publisher shall not be liable for any loss of profit, nor any personal or commercial damages, including but not limited to special, incidental, consequential, or other damages.

All rights reserved. No part of this book may be reproduced or transmitted in any form or by any means except as permitted under Section 107 or 108 of the 1976 United States Copyright Act and with written permission from the publisher. All materials are legal property of the author and Frisco House Publishing, LLC. Unauthorized duplication is strictly forbidden and punishable to the maximum extent under applicable law.

Publisher: Cargo Pocket Edition, A Division of Frisco House Publishing, LLC - Dallas, Texas

ISBN: 978-1-64370-383-1

Editor: Beverly Mansfield

Cover illustration and design: Brandon Triola

Printed in the United States of America

Copyright © 2018 by Brian C. Fleming
All rights reserved.

*To get more copies or order in bulk for your team or organization, go to: ResilienceBooklet.com or email us at: info@BrianCFleming.com.

TABLE OF CONTENTS

Read This First ... 7

CHAPTER 1
The Power of Self-Inflicted "Micro-Struggles" ... 13

CHAPTER 2
Lean, Don't Run ... 23

CHAPTER 3
Three Common Habits of the World's Most Resilient People ... 29

CHAPTER 4
The Upward Spiral ... 43

CHAPTER 5
Finding Closure and Confirmation ... 45

Do This... ... 51

DEDICATION

To all my fellow survivors who have experienced trauma, loss, or total life devastation and wondered if life was worth living, this book is for you. To those who suffer and struggle and just want to feel normal again but continue to wake up and battle every single day, you're not alone. We are all one human platoon of survivors, scattered across the earth and from all walks of life, who understand reality and pain from a perspective many never will. Your willingness to charge forward into your battle and continue to carry your load every day inspires me.

You're not alone. I believe in you. Your life is worth fighting for. You have what it takes..

READ THIS FIRST

My name is Brian, and this booklet is about resilience and how you can have more of it. I wrote this book for you. I wrote it to help you navigate beyond, and to win your life's toughest battles by applying a few of the top habits practiced by the world's most resilient people to your own life and circumstances. My hope is that after reading this short booklet you'll never have to suffer the pain of feeling isolated, stuck, lost, or alone again, especially if you have an experience that results in total life devastation.

I was inspired to write this book after returning home from a trip into Afghanistan as a civilian, six and a half years following my initial deployment, which resulted in a near-death experience in Kandahar. On this trip, I was reminded of how much gear a soldier must carry while on deployment and missions. Most of the time, they take only the essentials. After writing my second book, *Redeployed,* with my friend Chad Robichaux, I realized that I could create an equally valuable resource, but small, lightweight, and portable. Military service members (and you, as well) could carry this small book in the cargo pockets of their uniforms. I saw this idea as another way to help more people win their battles and overcome their daily struggles by getting this resource into their hands. The result is the book you are now holding in your hand.

Additionally, I travel countless thousands of miles across the globe every year as an author and professional speaker. I've discovered that although some people enjoy reading 600-page novels, others prefer a good, informative, and interesting book they can actually finish on a flight from Dallas to Los Angeles. A book this size is a cost-effective, faster, and easier way to spread a highly practical message of hope by getting it into the hands of more people who need it.

This book is not a philosophical analysis, a final solution, or an exhaustive doctoral thesis on the topic of suffering as it pertains to the human condition. I am not a Doctor of Psychology, nor do I desire to become one. Nothing in this book is meant to serve as a substitute or stop you from seeking professional help, if necessary. It is simply a part of the next step in the right direction for those who have suffered loss, trauma, injury, or other extreme pains or challenges. This book is an observation based on over 30 years of raw and painful life experiences. It is also the product of more than a decade of my personal study, practice, and teaching of principles of human resilience across the globe in colleges, universities, mental health organizations, associations of all kinds, Fortune 100 companies, and to the US Military.

Forgive me if the information in this book sounds all too simple. My mission is to help you win your life's toughest personal battles and move beyond your deepest, most devastating wounds in order to find peace and happiness again. I feel that is best accomplished by keeping this book as basic and conversational as possible, instead of exploring complex theories.

This book is not like others. It is blunt and direct for your benefit. It is just me talking to you, and I intentionally penned it this way. I have no desire to be perceived as any sort of "guru" who uses a bunch of fancy psychological lingo or uber-spiritual Jedi mind tricks to manipulate your thoughts into another state of confusion and frustration. Practicality and helping you get a desired outcome is the name of the game here. I'm not trying to win any awards for grammar or an impressive vocabulary, nor am I seeking to be recognized for any sort of scientific or philosophical breakthroughs.

Perhaps I've simply found an easier way to understand and explain a complex topic. At no point am I trying to impress you with what I've been able to overcome or done with my own life. I have no desire to merely project my life story onto yours. My only hope with this book is that I might contribute to the mass development of the most resilient, empathetic, authentic, and strongest generation our human race has ever produced—starting with you.

The way many extreme trauma survivors have overcome painful, devastating life experiences and moved forward has actually been quite simple. Not always easy, but simple. These easy-to-understand and practical concepts I'm going to share with you have worked wonders in my own life and the hundreds of thousands of people just like you I've had the honor of speaking to. If these simple ideas can make a difference for so many others (including myself), they can certainly make a difference in your life if you'll apply them. I want to equip you to reach a place in life where your inevitable pain and suffering, though uncomfortable, will become bearable, and your ability to move beyond those situations productively becomes second nature. If you have even a shred of belief that you can move beyond whatever horrifically painful, confusing, or paralyzing circumstance you've faced, this book is for you.

Chapter 1

THE POWER OF SELF-INFLICTED "MICRO-STRUGGLES"

Everybody gets hurt, but not everybody gets over it. Have you ever wondered why some people are able to endure unthinkably difficult circumstances and then prosper in spite of them, while others always seem to struggle and never move forward? There are many reasons. Every person and situation is unique, but I believe one of the primary reasons a lot of people are never able to overcome the trauma or pain they face is because we live in a society today that values comfort at all costs.

I think one of the greatest disservices we do for our kids, ourselves, and everybody around us is to encourage a comfortable life above all else and at all costs. A comfortable life should not be our ultimate goal (though it's obviously preferred), but rather we should strive to live a meaningful life. Each battle we struggle through and win builds our confidence, strength, and ability to handle future challenges. If you aren't comfortable with being uncomfortable, you can't develop the thick skin life will demand of you. This is why I often feel bad for people who have had easy lives—because they usually have no grit. I don't envy them. I'm not jealous of them. I'm glad they haven't suffered much because I care about them. But when the gun fights and explosions begin happening in my life, I won't be calling on those people for advice, and I wouldn't recommend you do it either. Instead, I seek out the people who are scarred up, the ones who, metaphorically, are wearing dirty, bloody, torn up body armor. Their life stories are war stories and testimonials of hard-won battles. Their stories tell me they've seen a thing or two and that they can offer me some sort of experienced guidance. When I'm in a fight, I want real, experienced, battle-hardened warriors to have my back.

All of this "fighting" and "warrior" talk may sound a bit weird to some, I know. But one of the greatest lessons the military ever taught me was to do something every day that sucks and to do it as early as possible. We didn't

The Power of Self-Inflicted "Micro-Struggles"

wake up at 4:00 a.m. to run five to ten miles (and more) for nothing. Doing something difficult first thing in the morning, every day, gives you a mental boost and sets you up for winning the battles you'll face throughout the rest of your day and the rest of your life.

As I write this to you, I'm at a hotel in Boston where I'll be speaking to over 400 mental health professionals on the topic of human resilience. I woke up at 5:00 a.m. this morning and ran for 35 minutes straight at about 80% sprint of my own pace to prep for my day. Nobody put a gun to my head. Nobody told me I had to do it. I was completely alone in the hotel gym at 5:00 a.m. (That's difficult to imagine, I know.) When doing the things that make you stronger and better, you may find yourself completely alone. Don't sweat it. That's just how the game of life is played. While the masses are asleep, slumbering in their beds, be the one who is up training for war. Then you will be more able to withstand the bloody, brutally violent attacks life will throw at you. It's one of the reasons I run four to seven miles every day and do Brazilian Jiu-Jitsu four or five times a week. Because it makes me struggle, and struggle produces strength.

In one of my workouts (not my daily run, but another workout I do about four days a week), a lady said to me, "Brian, I hate running." She then asked me, "Do you actually enjoy running?"

I replied, "No, running sucks."

She proceeded, "So why do you do it so much?"

I said, "Because it sucks."

She looked at me like I was speaking Chinese, like what I said to her didn't make any sense. And to be honest, it doesn't make much sense. But it works. Living your life with the intention and goal of becoming comfortably numb (so comfortable that everything is exactly how you'd ideally prefer it, all the time) defies the reality of how life is actually structured. Such a narrative is not the story of life. If you know anything about how great stories are crafted and told, they involve a character who wants something, but then tragedy usually strikes, and an obstacle stands in front of them. Then, the character has to figure out how to overcome the obstacle, and they don't usually know if they have what it takes to succeed. Their journey is filled with risk, uncertainty, loss, villains,

The Power of Self-Inflicted "Micro-Struggles"

betrayal, and all kinds of hidden dangers. Such is the story of your life and mine. To try and live our lives according to any other narrative is self-deceiving, denies reality, and is very damaging.

Fighting the war in Afghanistan and dealing with the aftermath, including the injuries I sustained from my vehicle getting blown up and then being attacked by a suicide bomber in Kandahar a few months later, were probably some of the greatest gifts I've ever received. It was the worst physical pain I've ever endured, and it hasn't been an easy road, but surviving that experience made me a better person.

When I look at the things I now do—the running, Brazilian Jiu-Jitsu, workouts, and everything else—I don't see these as mere fitness training. For me, they're survival training because I never know when I'm going to be on an airplane and some crazy person will act like a lunatic. I never know when someone will try to bomb a marathon. You never know what's going to happen in the course of your day-to-day activities. Life is completely unpredictable, and people who live with comfort as their ultimate goal are conditioning themselves for weakness and

The Resilience Booklet

defeat. When it comes time to step up and have some grit, if you aren't training for it little by little every day, you're just not going to have it. You can't buy grit. You can't borrow thick skin. You have to develop your own over time through varying degrees of struggle and conflict.

It's the same way we think and live in the military. We train and drill every possible war scenario thousands and thousands and thousands of times. Then, if we find ourselves in a battle when the bullets are real, we won't have to stand around and think about what to do. When life is happening to you in a really bad way, you don't always have time to think. You must be able to react, and if you're not trained up, you're not going to react in time. Life is like an ambush—you never know what you're going to face. If you get ambushed in the streets, you don't have time to stand around and think, "What should I do?" Because, if that's the case, you just got shot, stabbed, or punched while standing there trying to decide what to do.

We must train ourselves to react in certain ways to prepare for difficult situations. Now, you may be thinking, *But Brian, I'm not going to find myself in a gun fight or getting mugged in a dark alley any time soon*. I hope that's true.

There are two types of situations in life: situations we have control over and situations we do not have control over. The sooner we accept the fact that there are certain things we cannot control, the better off we will be. Even concerning the situations where we think we have control, it is actually very limited.

When we experience tough times, so much of the ultimate outcome is determined by our perception of our situation.

> *Your perception is the bridge between your place of pain and the place you're trying to get to.*

You can view your situation however you choose because your perception has to do with your belief system. It has to do with what you believe about your experience. Be sure to choose what you believe wisely. It will determine your ability to overcome massive challenges and successfully move forward.

Resilience is defined as "the ability to withstand, bounce back, or recover quickly and easily from shock, illness, adversity, hardship, or difficult conditions." Personally, I think resilience has less to do with bouncing back and a lot more to do with fighting forward. The world's most resilient people have no intention of going back and becoming the person they used to be. After all, they know and understand that what they've been through has changed them, and they'll never again be the person they once were. They know they can be better because of what they've endured.

When you experience trauma or hardship, your attitude needs to be about fighting through it, not crawling into a hole and hiding. When trying to move forward, it's not about avoiding anything and everything that reminds you of what you went through. That old demon of discomfort has a way of rearing its ugly head again and again to remind us of what happened; I know. It's uncomfortable to be reminded of our pain, no doubt. But avoiding our wounds and not dealing with them will only allow those wounds to become infected and hurt us longer. Instead of trying to avoid anything that reminds us of our pain, we should begin leaning into those things because familiarity breeds contentment. The more we revisit our place of pain

The Power of Self-Inflicted "Micro-Struggles"

(or prepare for an uncomfortable future situation that may arise), the more desensitized we tend to become towards it, and its ability to control us will weaken over time. Doing this can be very uncomfortable, but it's necessary and should be done cautiously and with support from others.

Chapter 2

LEAN, DON'T RUN

At the time of this writing, I've been doing Brazilian Jiu-Jitsu consistently four or five days a week for the past two and a half years. I work on it for at least an hour a day, sometimes twice a day. I was a beginner when I joined the gym, and every single day I'd go in and get my face slammed into the mat, tapped out, and nearly choked out (if I didn't tap). In fact, I even cracked a rib on my very first day of class! But I wasn't going to be denied this valuable life skill. If you don't know what Brazilian Jiu-Jitsu is, just watch the MMA fights on TV. When the fighters are on the ground pounding each other, that's pretty much Brazilian Jiu-Jitsu.

Why would I put myself in such a situation? Am I a glutton for punishment? Do I hate myself? Do I enjoy pain? No. But there's something philosophically interesting about that sport that has a lot to do with resilience, which you and I can both learn from. In the time I've been training, bigger and stronger guys have come and gone. I'm one of the smallest guys at my gym. I weigh about 170 pounds, and I'm six feet tall. We've had some very large people train at the gym, up to six feet five inches tall and weighing nearly 300 pounds.

One guy I rolled with was six foot four inches tall and weighed 270 pounds. He was a wrestler, and the guy was massive. If you were to stand us together and ask, "Who would win in a fight?" most people would likely point at the bigger guy. (I wouldn't blame them.) But I had an advantage. He was brand new to the sport, and I had been training for about six months when he arrived. As we began to spar, he charged me, and we went to the ground. About 45 seconds later, he was tapping his hand on the mat.

"What just happened? What happened?" he asked. As we went to the ground, I had thrown a leg over his shoulder and locked him into what's called a Triangle Choke (which is just a fancy way of saying I was choking him with my legs). He asked me to show him what I'd done, and so I did. I knew that it would make me better if he's trying to defend it next time.

Some people would say, "Wait, Brian! Don't give him your secrets. Don't tell him how you did it." No, I gave him my secret because I knew it would make me work harder and become better. Struggle is the only thing that has ever produced real strength, so you might as well put yourself through it in a safe, controlled environment. It will prepare you for the real thing, whether Brazilian Jiu-Jitsu or any other real-life situation.

I meet a lot of guys in that sport who are bigger and stronger than me, as you can imagine. Many of them have always been the alpha male in their circles of influence because of their physical size and strength, but when many of them get into a situation where a person half their size can defeat them quickly, some leave and never come back. And that's the worst thing they could do. It's also the worst thing you and I can do when we face a setback or loss. When struggle or hardship comes into your life, don't merely run from it or deny its existence. Instead, lean into it. Embrace it and learn how to defeat it.

When you get hit hard by life, don't quit on yourself. Don't get up, walk out the door, and never come back. The better thing to do is to come back the next day and learn how to defend against the thing that beat you last time. Brazilian Jiu-Jitsu is a great teacher and great metaphor for life. There's something eerily profound about the sport because when you're in a situation where somebody just "got you" and you know you can't get out of it, it's very primal and very disturbing. Your inner dialogue basically says, "If this was a life and death fight, I would have just lost," and that is an extremely uncomfortable feeling. That is a feeling nobody ever wants to experience. The best thing you can do in such a training situation is press through the discomfort and keep showing up day after day because you become better, stronger, and more confident at handling those tough, uncomfortable situations by doing so.

I've often wondered to myself, *What if I'm on the street, or on a date with my wife, and we get cornered by somebody? Maybe this person is on drugs or they're just having a bad day and they want to pound me or hurt my wife?* This scenario happens multiple times in our society every single day. There are crazy, evil people in this world. I've always figured that if I may find myself in that situation someday, I might as well be prepared for it. Consequently, that decision had more to do with me leaning into situations that are extremely uncomfortable than it did with me trying to avoid those situations all together—which just isn't entirely possible.

When you lean into your struggles, instead of avoiding them, you become stronger and are more likely to win the battles you will eventually face. Strength and small victories over time produce confidence. Confidence can lead you to victory.

Chapter 3

THREE COMMON HABITS OF THE WORLD'S MOST RESILIENT PEOPLE

I've learned there is a difference between people who are able to successfully overcome tragedy and trauma and those who aren't. People have asked me for years, as I get up and speak to audiences, "Brian, what was the *ONE THING* that made the difference in your life and allowed you to overcome the devastating tragedy you faced?"

I don't think there is any "one thing" that was a magic solution, and for years I didn't actually know what had made the difference in my life. One thing I do know is that I'm now living in a "new normal." Life will never return to the way it once was, and I've chosen to accept life as it is now. The faster you can do that in your own life, the better off you'll be. I've never tried to go back to the Brian I used to be because the Brian I am now is so much better, wiser, and stronger. I couldn't be who I am and enjoy the life I do today if all the horrible things in my past had not happened to me.

What made the difference and allowed me, and so many other extreme tragedy survivors, to move forward beyond our pain and setbacks? There are three foundational qualities we all seem to have in common. We have many more, but these are the most notable. Fortunately for you, none of us inherited or were born with these qualities. They are learned, which means you can learn, develop, and apply them to your own life and situation to overcome and win your own battles.

1. MEANING

The first thing I realized the world's most resilient people all had in common was that even while enduring tough times, and in the aftermath of their plight, they all had a strong sense of meaning about their suffering. They either believed their suffering was for a higher purpose and/or they had hope that their suffering would at some point come to an end. Our sense of meaning is tied directly to our belief system, which is core to

Three Common Habits of the Most Resilient People

our being. At the end of the day, you and I are going to believe exactly what we choose to believe about life, God, our circumstances, other people, etc. It's entirely up to us and our outcomes—as well as the quality of our lives—will be determined by what we believe about our experiences. Believing that good could come from the second and third-degree burns on my hands, face, and neck, the Post-Traumatic Stress, and a traumatic brain injury—which impaired my attention span, gave me debilitating headaches every day, and impaired my short-term memory—wasn't easy. But I chose to believe it anyway.

After surviving the suicide bombing in Afghanistan, my recovery at Brooke Army Medical Center (BAMC) lasted 14 months. BAMC was a place of healing, but also a horrible place of death and indescribable pain. There were good men and women in hospital rooms next to mine, horrifically injured in war, who never made it out of that hospital alive.

Throughout my time at BAMC, I always believed that my suffering was for a reason, even though I didn't know what that reason was. I continued my recovery in that state of mind even after leaving the hospital. Was I full of faith? Sure, I made a simple choice to believe. Was I being delusional? Perhaps, but I don't think so. The types of explosions I had survived in Afghanistan were usually fatal. I chose to believe there was a greater reason for me surviving and made it my mission to find out why. I decided the experience wasn't going to be the end of my life, but a new beginning. As far as I was concerned, I was starting a new chapter of my life. I was going to be comfortable with the discomfort while exploring and embracing my journey of discovery, and try to search out the ultimate reason for my survival.

One of the most daunting challenges of searching for meaning in our pain and struggles is that we never know if we're actually going to find it. And if we do, we don't know if it will take six months or 60 years. But one thing I've learned to be true is that those who are willing to search for something long enough usually end up finding it, sometimes in places and in ways they least expect.

One of the people who helped me make the most sense of my painful situation after coming home from Afghanistan was a man named Viktor Frankl. He was an Austrian Jew and psychiatrist during World War II. He lost

Three Common Habits of the Most Resilient People

most of his family in the Nazi concentration camps, but Dr. Frankl survived and went on to live a very productive, successful life after he was liberated by American forces and the war ended. In the months and years following my devastating war injury, I struggled to clearly describe to people how I was able to move forward beyond my mental and physical barriers so quickly and start living a happy, fulfilling life again. I just sort of did it. When people asked how I was able to do it, I never knew what to say. But what I didn't know how to communicate in 10,000 words, Dr. Frankl was able to sum up in a single sentence in his book, *Man's Search for Meaning*: He said, "In some ways, suffering ceases to be suffering at the moment it finds a meaning."

Let's look at that again: "In some ways, suffering ceases to be suffering at the moment it finds a meaning." In other words, when we begin to find meaning in our suffering, it actually transforms and becomes something else. Our suffering then becomes a sort of asset which transcends us.

I didn't know the ultimate meaning behind my horrific war injury—if there was one—or if I'd ever find it, but I still pursued it anyway. Consequently, something happened. About five months after arriving at BAMC, a man I'd never met showed up at the hospital. His name was Dave. He was my first mentor, and to this day, he is one of my best friends. He is a Vietnam veteran who was horribly injured in combat. He was on a river boat with Naval Special Warfare units in Vietnam. Dave was poised to throw a phosphorus grenade into some brush on the river bank when a sniper, aiming for his head, shot his hand, piercing the phosphorous grenade just inches from his right ear. It instantly burned about half the skin off his body. Thirty-seven years later, he came to BAMC and spoke to me and 30 other guys who were burned up, missing arms, legs, eyes, and more. He talked to us about how to continue moving forward beyond our injuries and gave us hope.

A lot of people may have seen him as just another injured war veteran, but I saw something different. I saw a guy who was just like me. He understood the pain I was dealing with because he'd experienced it himself decades earlier. I saw a guy who used to be where I was, but he didn't stay there. I thought to myself, *If I can learn nothing else from this guy, he can show me how to get out of this because he's done it.*

Three Common Habits of the Most Resilient People

What does this have to do with finding a sense of meaning and moving forward beyond our suffering? Everything.

I met Dave on January 25, 2007, a few months after my injury. About a month after meeting him, I received a call from his secretary. She told me Dave was speaking in Manhattan, Kansas, near the Fort Riley Army Base and invited me to attend his event. I showed up. He had reserved a seat for me in the front row. Right in the middle of his talk, he walked to the front of the stage, looked down, pointed at me, and said, "Brian, come on up here. Tell 'em about yourself!"

The auditorium had filled up since I'd taken my seat, and as I walked on stage, I realized there were about 3,000 people in the audience! I was still wrapped up in burn bandages at the time. My face was still slightly pink and red from the second-degree burns. I spoke for about two minutes and said something like, "Hi, I'm Brian. I got blown up. I guess I'm still here for a reason."

Although a good opportunity, that experience didn't change my life. What changed the course of my life forever was what happened when I walked off stage. It's what I call the "game changer." It's the one-degree shift that changed everything for me and a lot of my fellow tragedy and trauma survivors who have had similar experiences. After exiting the stage, a young lady walked up to me and said, "Hey Brian, I was raped and abused and molested growing up." She continued, "My boyfriend was abusive in the same ways, he just broke up with me, and I tried to kill myself but failed."

I didn't know what to say to her, and I didn't know why she was telling me these intimate details of her life. But she ended our conversation by saying this: "Brian, if you can get through your horrible war injury, I think I can get through this. If God can bring you through your struggle, I think He can bring me through mine."

Wow! Suddenly, that suicide bombing, the war in Afghanistan, the explosions, long missions, everything that led me up to that point, including the daily headaches, traumatic brain injury, post-traumatic stress, and burn treatments all began to have a sense of meaning. My suffering, I realized, had become an asset I'd used (unknowingly) to help and convince a young lady not to attempt to kill herself again. My suffering suddenly became purpose driven. I discovered meaning in my suffering, as Dr. Frankl would describe it, and it became something else. It became a source of hope, strength, and good for others who are suffering.

Sometimes our pain is so intense and difficult to ignore that we can't seem to think of anything or anyone else. But much healing is found when we put our own pain on pause for a moment and reach out to help others heal and win their battles. Meaning is never found by looking within and focusing on ourselves, though we can learn some valuable lessons by doing so. Meaning is more often found in what we actively do to help ease the pain and suffering of others with the assets we have to offer.

2. MENTORS

The second thing the world's most resilient people have in common is mentors. If you look at anybody who has been through an extremely traumatic, painful, or challenging experience and recovered well from it, they usually had somebody in their life to help them. Somebody—or perhaps a number of people—mentored them through their experience. In the military, we have a chain of command. You have somebody above you, beside you, and below you. Sometimes it can even be multiple people in each position. There are those you follow who can lead and guide you. There are those who are on your same level who are walking the journey with you. And there are those you're tasked with leading, contributing to, and investing in. I call this a "personal chain of command."

If you look at almost any extreme trauma survivor who was able to successfully recover and move forward, you'll see that they usually had all three types of these people in their lives at one time or another, and it contributed to helping them move forward. It's not necessary for these people in your life to have gone through the same painful experiences you have. They just need to care about you, offer a different or better perspective on your situation, and offer some guidance about how to take your next step forward.

Some people believe that only those who have "been in their shoes" can help them and nobody else is qualified to do so. This is ignorance to the highest degree. But contrary to this commonly held belief, sometimes other people who have been through the same bad experiences as you can be the least helpful.

Three Common Habits of the Most Resilient People

Why? One reason is because their perspective is often, but not always, inhibited by the same fog that is keeping you stuck. It may be the people you least expect—people who have never endured a pain like yours—who are able to help you the most because their perspective has not been tainted by having had the same experience as you. Other people's perspectives can be so different than your own that they can often see barriers holding you back that you can't see because you are too close to your own situation. In a wartime scenario, this is referred to as "the fog of war."

Don't be afraid to reach out for help when you need it. Instead of listening to your ego and thinking, *I don't want to look weak by asking for help,* or *I can handle this on my own*, follow the battle-proven tactics that military leaders have used for centuries that actually work and help win wars.

In war, a platoon commander whose small unit is under heavy attack would never deny air support (attack helicopters and war planes) that are readily available to help his platoon win a battle and get out alive. When offered assistance, a good commander would never reply: "We don't want your help. You don't know what it's like down here on the ground. The enemy is fierce and quick, and things are bad, but we've got this!" No soldier would respect a leader who is too insecure, too weak, and too egotistical to accept help when it's needed. Don't be that person in your own war story. Nobody is impressed. If you need help, be smart enough to call in air support (friends, advisors, and mentors). That's why they exist. The world's most resilient people all have mentors who help them move forward.

3. MISSION

The third thing the world's most resilient people have in common is that they're usually living for the accomplishment of a mission greater than themselves.

The mission is the greater purpose, which transcends yourself and your own personal credit, glory, or gain. It's what you've bought in and sold out to and want to accomplish.

The mission is the action piece of your daily life, and it usually proves and reinforces the "meaning" a person claims they're living for. It's what you're working toward and living

Three Common Habits of the Most Resilient People

for every day. A mission always has a clearly defined, desired outcome and is backed by action.

My personal life mission is to help people win their inner battles by teaching them principles of human resilience, so they can live happily and productively beyond trauma. One way I do this is by giving speeches and sharing information through books and products such as this one. I claim this is what I stand for. But if I'm not doing something, if I'm not speaking or writing books, or doing something else that proves my proclaimed meaning, it would be very easy not to believe me, and that mission would ultimately fail (and so would I).

This applies to everybody. It's the same reason most people don't like politicians. In general, politicians are thought to say anything that will get them elected and then do whatever they want once elected. Oftentimes, the meaning a politician claims to be campaigning for does not align with his or her actions once in office. Don't be that person in your own story. Find something greater than yourself that you genuinely care about and want to work toward every day that you're willing to sacrifice, and even die for, because you're so deeply committed to it and believe in it. It must be something greater to live for than yourself and your own personal gain or recognition. Make your mission simple and clear to understand and never stop taking action toward its accomplishment.

Chapter 4

THE UPWARD SPIRAL

Something incredible will begin to transform on the inside when you begin applying these three habits used by the world's most resilient people to your own daily life and circumstances. You'll find yourself living a very different, and better, story when you have a strong sense of meaning in your experiences, are aligned with and supported by good people on all sides, and are working towards, and living for, the accomplishment of a mission that transcends you. Instead of experiencing a downward spiral where one bad thing contributes to another and leads to all sorts of destructive outcomes, you'll start experiencing more of an "upward" spiral because these three foundational principles of human resilience will all be active and contributing to one another in and through your life.

RECAP

The three common habits of the world's most resilient people are:

1. Meaning

2. Mentors

3. Mission

If you'd like me to personally walk you through this process, step-by-step, so you can come back from your setbacks a stronger and better person, simply join me right now at:

www.TakeBackYourLife.me

Chapter 5

FINDING CLOSURE AND CONFIRMATION

When you live according to the foundational principles of human resilience explained in this book, not only will you enjoy a more fulfilling life with stronger relationships, more opportunities, and a greater sense of purpose, but you'll also enjoy periodic, unforeseen confirmations that will make your life rich with a deep sense of meaning. I've probably experienced a dozen of these "unforeseen confirmations" over the past decade and each one has solidified my resolve to live strong, live well, and keep moving forward, no matter what I'm facing. One such experience took place seven years following my combat injury in Afghanistan, and I've never been the same since.

I had the opportunity to go back to Afghanistan in 2013, years after I'd been officially discharged from the military. As a civilian, I wasn't permitted to carry a weapon, which I was not thrilled about because the last time I was in Afghanistan I had plenty of weapons and still almost died. But I chose to go anyway. While in the country, I had the chance to speak with troops who had been deployed there for months, many of whom were on their fourth and fifth deployments. The entire time I was there, I kept wondering, *Why did this opportunity to return to Afghanistan really present itself?* The whole thing was just odd. I thought, *Surely, there must be a reason.* I had a feeling that there was something bigger (unseen) going on that I wasn't able to yet see but would soon realize.

We arrived in Afghanistan. I was there for an entire week, and in that time and through all of the experiences we had, I couldn't seem to find any rhyme or reason as to why this opportunity had presented itself. It bothered me. Call me super-spiritual or call me what you want. I had a deep suspicion, for reasons unknown to me, that I'd find something out about myself on this journey back into the place where I'd been hurt.

After seven days of traveling across the war-torn nation of Afghanistan by way of airplanes, Black Hawk helicopters, and armored vehicles, we boarded a military aircraft and flew out of Bagram Airfield. Hours later, we landed in Kuwait City where we had a long layover before our connecting flight departed back to the US. At this point, I was quite puzzled because something inside of me felt undone. It was like a story loop had been opened inside of me but hadn't been resolved and closed. It bothered me.

About an hour before we were to depart for the airport and fly home, something happened. I was walking back from a small store near the place our vehicles were parked. Suddenly, from my "seven o'clock" (slightly behind me and to my left) about 30 feet away, someone yelled, "Hey, Sergeant Fleming!"

Who the heck knows me here? Who even knows I'm here? I didn't even tell my mother I was coming back here. Who recognizes me? I wondered all of this in a micro-second of confusion. I'd been walking with a group of other soldiers all wearing the Army multicam camouflage uniform, headgear, and sunglasses. In other words, we all looked identical. Picking me out of that crowd was nearly impossible.

The Resilience Booklet

A man in uniform came running up. It was my friend, Mike, the man who had pulled my half-dead, burned up body from our blasted, burning vehicle after the suicide bombing in Afghanistan seven years prior! Mike and I hadn't seen each other since that day. This was the guy who saved my life. The last time he'd seen me I was a burned, bloody mess. And now here we were, crossing paths as we walked down the street in a peaceful Middle Eastern country. Our chance encounter ended up turning into a big story featured in the *Army Times* (totally unplanned, obviously). But the real beauty in the story is that Mike and I had the opportunity to talk for about an hour and pick up our conversation where we'd left off seven years prior.

Mike explained that after the day we were hit by the suicide bomber, he didn't quite feel like himself. The experience had changed him in ways that took time for him to fully understand. After all, he had not only saved me, but also our 19-year-old gunner who was burned, peppered with shrapnel, and lost his right eye in the attack. As we sat and talked, I prodded him for more details. It seemed that he felt responsible and guilty about our young gunner being wounded so badly. He thought that he should have been the one up on the gun in the turret and injured by the blast. I was totally shocked by his statement because as a combat medic, Mike had performed his duties under fire flawlessly and saved our lives. He had pulled two severely wounded men from his burning vehicle, treated and stabilized us, called in the medical evacuation (Med-Evac) helicopter, and then immediately returned to duty following the incident.

Recalling the event from my own perspective, I was quick to remind Mike that we had agreed at the beginning of that mission that he would drive the vehicle because he knew the route to our destination better than any of us, and our younger soldier would be best up on the gun. That was a decision we made together, and given the same scenario, any good commander would've made the same decision. I told him, "Mike, it wasn't your fault. You made the right decision."

I didn't know this until later, but he told the *Army Times* reporter, "Brian understands what it was like that day because we experienced that hell together. I know Brian won't judge me for anything because he knows what it was like. He was there. When Brian told me that I'd made the right decision that day, seven years of guilt lifted off of my shoulders."

Please understand that I'm not the hero in this story—Mike is. (He would deny it, but it's the truth.) After our brief reunion, I boarded a plane and flew back to the US. While droning in and out of sleep on our long flight home, I suddenly realized something: I hadn't gone back into Afghanistan to discover something about myself, as I'd originally thought. Without realizing it, I'd gone back into Afghanistan for Mike. I was supposed to see him that day and play a vital role in the next step of his healing journey. This encounter with Mike reaffirmed a great and deep sense of meaning in the tragic, but beautiful, story of my life.

The greatest healing is often found when we are finally able to focus outside of ourselves and help other people win their own battles—even if it requires us going back into the place that hurt us the most—so we can play an unforeseen role in the healing journey of our friends on our way out.

DO THIS

Before you put this book down, I want you to go through a simple checklist to get the most out of this book and out of yourself. Knowing this information isn't enough. Applying it to your life or circumstances daily starting right now is what will transform your life for the better.

SIMPLY DO THESE THINGS RIGHT NOW

- **If you want me to personally** give you further, step-by-step guidance on how to easily apply these concepts to your everyday life, so you can overcome your challenges faster and live a more meaningful and fulfilling life, simply go to:

    www.TakeBackYourLife.me

- **Keep *The Resilience Booklet*** with you everywhere you go until you move beyond your current challenge or obstacle. When you do, make me the first person you contact so I can celebrate with you.

- **Gift a fresh new copy** of *The Resilience Booklet* to someone you care about who is fighting a battle of their own. If we care, we share. Pay it forward! Grab a copy for a friend at:

    www.ResilienceBooklet.com

- **Take a selfie** with your copy of *The Resilience Booklet* and tag me on Facebook and Instagram, so you and I can personally connect:

    @BrianCFleming
    #ResilienceBooklet

You are stronger than you think you are. You have what it takes. Go get after it!

— Brian

Your next step is to join me at Take Back Your Life Online!

Do it now.

MOVE BEYOND THE PAIN FROM YOUR PAST AND ENJOY EVERYDAY LIFE

ONLINE RESILIENCE PROGRAM

A Step-by-Step Online Video Series That Shows You How to Take Back Your Power!

3 SIMPLE STEPS

1) Watch The Videos
2) Fill in the Blanks
3) *Live a Meaningful Life*

Get started now at
TakeBackYourLife.ME

BATTLE PLAN FOR LIFE

TRANSFORM YOUR LIFE!

The Live Workshop That Helps You Take Your Next Step & Finally Move Forward Using Proven Military War Strategies

Gain Expert Insight | **Create a Plan That Works** | **Get The Results In Life You Want**

Our workshops help you craft an individually-designed success plan for getting from where you are to where you want to be!

"This program is unlike any other! It's a simple framework for overcoming adversity and living in victory!"
- CHAD WILLIAMS, US Navy SEAL

Learn more and sign up for a FREE training at:
BattlePlanForLife.com

ABOUT THE AUTHOR

BRIAN FLEMING is a Combat-Wounded Afghanistan War Veteran, Author, Speaker & Resilience Trainer. He was awarded the Purple Heart after being severely wounded in combat by a suicide bomber who exploded 3-feet away from him in Kandahar. Following 14 months at a medical center, he rebuilt his life from the ground up. Now, he helps organizations develop more resilient leaders who thrive under pressure by teaching them his hard-won life lessons about human resilience and succeeding beyond unexpected challenges. He has delivered hundreds of presentations to over half-a-million people in live audiences across 42 US states, in 7 countries, and on 4 continents. His client list ranges from small businesses, churches, and network marketing organizations to trade associations, colleges, the US Military, and Fortune 500 companies. Because of his expertise, he is a frequently sought after guest of the news media and has been featured on every major news network in North America. He is the author of 4 books and lives near Dallas, TX.

Brian's work has been featured on

FOX   CNN   abc   CBS   CNBC   ESPN   USA TODAY   THE HUFFINGTON POST

To learn more about having Brian speak at your next event and help your organization develop more resilient leaders who thrive under pressure, visit: **BrianCFleming.com**

LISTEN TO THE WIN YOUR BATTLES PODCAST

 Apple Podcasts
★★★★★

RATED 5-STARS IN LEADERSHIP ON ITUNES

AVAILABLE ON:
- Listen on Apple Podcasts
- GET IT ON Google Play
- STITCHER
- Spotify